SILVER LINING
(Crazy 'Bout You)

Words and Music by
DIANE WARREN

Rubato

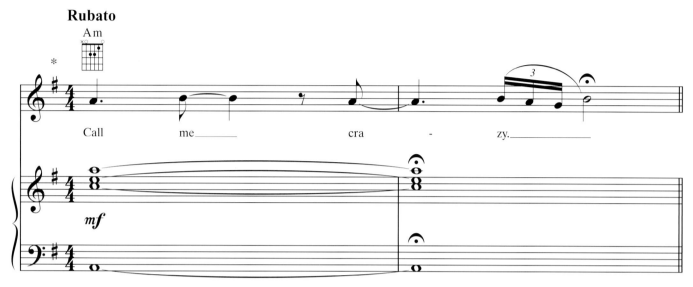

Call me_____ cra - zy._____

Moderate pop rock ♩ = 100

Verse 1:

1. In a world where no one, no one un - der - stands,_____ it's good to fin - 'lly find some -

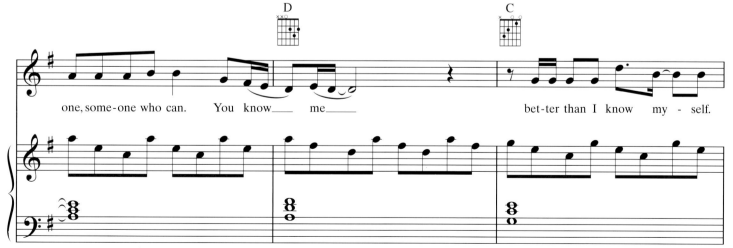

one, some-one who can. You know_____ me_____ bet-ter than I know my - self.

*Original recording in F♯ major.